Contents

Chapter I. Introduction

Chapter II. Theoretical Foundation of Public Welfare Schemes

Chapter III. Financial Inclusion & Analysis

Chapter IV. Conclusion

Chapter I: Introduction to MGNREGA

Introduction: Mahatma Gandhi National Rural Employment Guarantee Act, 2005

India has a huge proportion of its population living in villages and the rural character of the country is reflected in the Govt. of India Census 2011, which shows that 69% of Indians live in rural areas. Besides, India is home to one third of the poor people in the world who are living below international poverty line of $1.90 a day *(World Bank, 2016)*. The rural character of India coupled with massive poverty in the country, policy makers have given considerable importance to poverty alleviation, unemployment reduction and economic development particularly in rural areas. These objectives are a common focus in all the five-year plans formulated since independence in 1947. The setting up of planning commission in 1950 was a major milestone in this direction as it laid down the objectives and strategies for economic development of India with special attention given to rural economy *(Desai, 2009)*.

The importance and attention given to employment generation is not new in the world. The programmes to ensure employment to poor dates back to The Poor Employment Act of 1817 and 1834 Poor Law Amendment Act in Great Britain *(Balaug, 1964, Clément, 2011)* and the New Deal program of the 1930s in the United States *(Rosenof, T, 1987)* were considered relief policies during economic slowdown. The programmes focusing on employment generation, poverty reduction, sustainable assets creation and increasing per-capita incomes are being followed both in advanced and developing economies. The countries that have implemented such programmes in the past are Chile (1987), Pakistan (1992), Bangladesh (1983), Philippines (1990), Botswana (1960), Kenya (1992) and Thailand.

India in its attempt to ensure employment generation, poverty reduction, assets creation and reasonable standard of living for its people particularly in rural areas various important rural development schemes have been launched in the past. The rural development schemes include Community Development Programme (CDP) of 1952, Small Farmers Development Agency (1969-70), Marginal Farmers and Agricultural Labourers Programme (MFAL) (1969-70), Integrated Rural Development Programme (IRDP) (1976-77), Food For Work Programme (FWP) (1977), Training Rural Youth For Self-Employment (TRYSEM) (1979), Rural Employment Programme (1980), Jawahar Rozgar Yojana (1989), Swaranjayanti Gram

Swarozgar Yojana (SGSY) (1999) & National Food For Work Programme (2004). All of these programmes however suffered from various loopholes viz. lack of awareness among local communities, little involvement of the local community, employment was provided based on availability of funds & willingness of the implementation machinery and lack of social monitoring. The outcome was wastage of resources, leakages and corruption, inability to provide minimum livelihood security as there was no guarantee, low allocation and utilization of funds, less number of days of wage employment per family, lack of right planning, creation of low quality assets, involvement of contractors and use of machinery, false muster rolls etc. Thus, all these programmes failed to achieve the set objectives. To overcome the problems of earlier wage employment programmes, Government of India took a major policy decision by enacting the National Rural Employment Guarantee Act (NREGA) in 2005 by merging Swaranjayanti Gram Rozgar Yojana (SGRY) & National Food For Work Programme (NFFWP) for providing livelihood security to rural unemployed and the Act was subsequently rechristened in 2009 as MGNREGA. The Act was introduced in India to guarantee employment for those who are willing to do unskilled wage employment at the prevailing minimum wage rate in a particular state *(MGNREGA, 2005-06)*. It is a policy of direct transfer to the poor through the provision of public works *(Drèze and Sen, 1991; von Braun, 1995, Lipton 1996)* satisfying the property of self-selection.

The enactment of MGNREGA (2005-06), a flagship rural development programme of Govt. of India, is a rights based approach to rural development which was missing in previous rural development schemes *(Anand c, 2014)*. It is aimed at providing livelihood security in rural India by providing work on demand to the rural households to do unskilled work for a period of 100 days at the prevailing minimum wage rate in the states *(MGNREGA Act, 2005)*. The focus of MGNREGA is on creating sustainable rural livelihood through regeneration of the natural resource base by creation of durable assets, enhancing productivity and strengthening rural governance through decentralized planning & built in system of accountability in the form of social audits *(MGNREGA Act, 2005)*.

The MGNREGA ranks among the most powerful policy interventions for the socio-economic uplifment of rural India. The MGNREGA has three distinct goals including protective, preventive and promotive. It protects the rural poor from vulnerabilities by providing them demand based employment. It prevents risks associated with agricultural investment and forced migration of the rural poor. It brings in buoyancy in rural economy via increased consumption demand *(Mathur, 2007)*.

The MGNREGA provides basis for permanent social security system and even acts as an instrument for planned and equitable rural development. It also focuses on raising the productivity of agriculture by creating durable assets. To ensure rights and entitlements of workers under MGNREGA, an exclusive National Rural Employment Guarantee Fund has been set up for implementation of the programme. The Act has a systematic approach for identification and execution of works and payment of wages. It also has the provision for transparency and accountability of implementing agencies. The direct outcome of this provision is conduct of social audits by the Gram Sabhas (GSs) which have been mandated not only by Right to Information (RTI) Act but also the MGNREGA Act 2005-06.

The J&K state has extended the benefits of the central act to the rural areas in the state in a phased manner by framing its own policy known as Mahatma Gandhi National Rural Employment Guarantee Scheme (MGNREGS). This was done to overcome the constitutional limitations as the central MGNREGA is not applicable to the state. Therefore, the present study uses the acronym MGNREGS instead of MGNREGA.

MGNREGA Time Line

Table 1.1: Evolution of MGNREGA

Aug. 2005	Feb. 2006	April 2007	April 2008	Oct. 2008	Feb. 2009	Oct. 2009	Source:
NREGA Legalized	Implemented in 200 Districts in India	Additional 130 districts included	Universal Implementation in India	Wage transfer through bank/ post office	MOU with postal department	MGNREGA nomenclature adopted	*www.nrega.nic.in*

The Salient features of the MGNREGA Act and a list of Permissible Activities under the Act is given at **Appendix I & Appendix II** respectively.

Research Gap

There are several research studies which have focused on the impact of the scheme in India. Besides, the previous studies have also attempted to analyze the implementation and process mechanism of the scheme in India for past many years which have been extensively reviewed in a separate chapter on literature review. However, there has been no research attempt made till date to study the operational efficacy of MGNREGS in the study area. There has also been no research conducted on testing the self-targeting design of the scheme. Besides, previous studies have mostly depended on descriptive statistical tools to analyze the impact of the scheme in India. The present study is an attempt to bridge this research gap in the literature by empirically examining the operational efficacy of MGNREGS in-terms of its impact on key performance indicators such as man-days generated or employment, addition to household income, financial inclusion of beneficiary rural households, rural-urban migration, awareness regarding various entitlements/ provisions of the scheme and participation of rural households. The study also tries to analyze the self targeting design of the study by examining the effect of socio-economic profile of beneficiaries on the participation in MGNREGS scheme. The present study has also relied on robust statistical tools both parametric and non-parametric to draw inferences and conclusions.

Research Methodology

A combination of exploratory and descriptive research design is used for conducting this study. The study has relied on a multi-stage random sampling design for drawing a representative sample from the study area. The data has been drawn from both primary and secondary sources for the purpose of hypotheses testing. The selection of blocks was done on the basis of a ranking scale based on key performance indicators adopted from *Prasana.V, 2014* with slight modification to reflect the distinct socio-economic characteristics of the study area.

Sampling Design

A **Multi-Stage Random Sampling Design** has been adopted in the study to generate a representative sample for data collection and hypotheses testing. In **the First stage**, two districts (Kupwara and Poonch) of J&K State were selected from the Phase-I MGNREGS districts on the basis of socio-economic profile. These two districts are among the poorest districts in J&K state. Poonch district is the poorest district in Jammu division with 33.67% & Kupwara is the poorest district in Kashmir division with 32.55% BPL population *(JK BPL Survey, 2008)*. Besides, Poonch has an average population per branch of 14000 people making it the most backward district on financial inclusion followed by Kupwara *(JK Economic Survey, 2014)*. On the basis of average land holding size of households; Poonch has an average land holding size of 0.88 hectares while Kupwara has an average land holding size of 0.46 hectares which is lower than the state average land holding size of 0.67 Hectare (Agricultural Census 2010-11).

In the **Second Stage,** Four blocks with two each from Poonch & Kupwara were selected for the present research study. The consolidated data on key indicators for various blocks in sample districts was downloaded from the website www.nrega.nic.in for FY 2014-15. For each selected indicator, performance score was given based on weightage as indicated below:

- Average days of employment provided to each participating household – 25 per cent weightage.

- Average days of employment provided to SC, OBC & ST households – 15 per cent weightage.

- Percentage of participation of women – 15 per cent weightage.

- Percentage works completed out of total works taken up for execution – 15 per cent weightage.

- Percentage of participating households completed 100 days of employment – 15 per cent weightage.

- Percentage of job card holding household participation in MGNREGS work – 15 per cent weightage *(Prasana V. 2014)*.

Thus, all the blocks in sample districts (Phase-I) were given indicator wise scores and then based on overall score, ranking was given to each block. Accordingly, on the basis of performance, two blocks in each district were selected for the purpose of the study.

In the **Third Stage,** Halqa Panchayats (HPs) were selected on the basis of their performance. The list of halqa panchayats in selected districts was collected from block development office (BDO) and a total of four Halqa Panchayts were selected from the sample blocks.

In the **Fourth stage,** the selection of households (HH's) was made. The households were selected on the basis of their participation in MGNREGS works. The households that have participated for two or more years were selected to assess the operational efficacy of MGNREGS. The list of participating households was downloaded from the website and the households which have participated for more than 2 years were randomly selected for the purpose of the study. While selecting these households, care has been taken to cover all habitations of selected halqa panchayats. In each Halqa Panchayat, 50 MGNREGS participating households were selected. Thus, the total sample size covered in the study is 200 Households (HH's).

The sample households have been randomly selected from a largely homogenous population as all the rural households irrespective of their socio-economic background are employed in unskilled wage employment for a maximum of 100 days in a year at prevailing minimum wage rate in the state. Therefore, keeping in view the representativeness of the sample, a sample size of 200 HH's have been randomly selected from the four halqa panchayats in two districts of J&K. Further, various studies have been conducted on the impact of MGNREGS with a much smaller sample size of 160 HH's, 160 HH's & 100 Households (HH's) *(PRASANNA V, 2014, Rashmi B, 2013 & Palanichamy, A.P, 2011).*

Figure 1.1 Sample Design of the Study

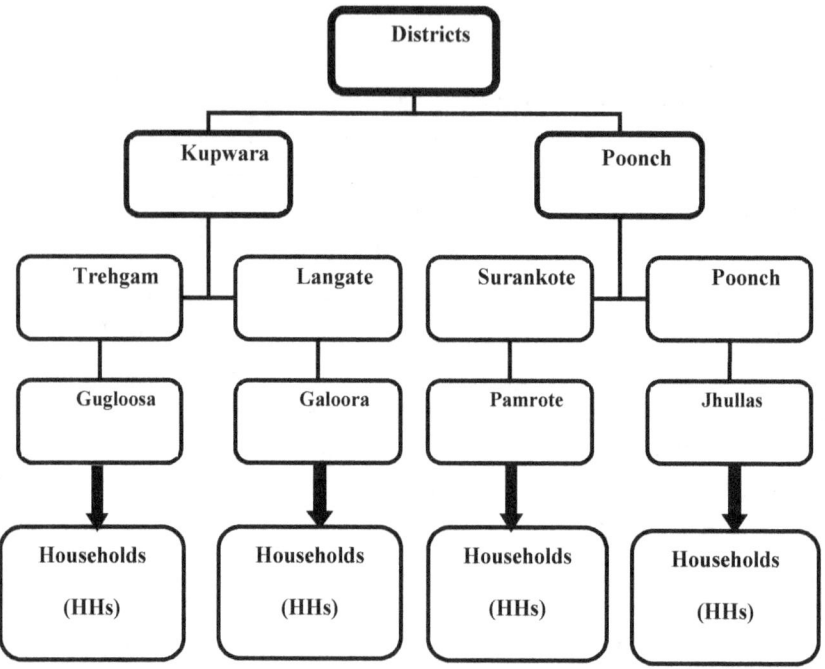

1.5.2 Scope of the Study

The scope of the study is limited to analyzing the operational efficacy of MGNREGS in terms of its impact on wage employment, incomes of beneficiary respondents, migration, awareness and participation of rural households and financial inclusion of the participants. The study aims to analyze the operational efficacy of the scheme in terms of its impact in Kupwara and Poonch districts of Jammu & Kashmir. The study is limited to analysis of 200 randomly selected beneficiary households in four halqa panchayats in the study area. The reference period for this study is from 2009-10 to 2015-16.

Methodology for Data Collection

A survey methodology has been adopted to achieve the objectives of the study and for testing of hypotheses. The data collection was done with the help of survey schedule/questionnaire in sample districts of Poonch and Kupwara of Jammu & Kashmir. The secondary data for the present study was collected between 2009-10 to 2015-16 whereas the primary data was collected in 2014-15. The primary data was collected using schedule/questionnaire which was pre-tested before initiating field survey in the selected districts so as to check the reliability of the survey instrument in capturing the required data. The reliability was checked for likert scale data using Cronbach's Alpha with >.70 considered reliable (Nunally, 1978 & Haier et al, 2006). The tools given below were used for generating data from the study area:

- Household Survey Questionnaire/schedule (HSQ) targeting participants or beneficiaries for data collection.
- Other modes of primary data collection: worksite visits, review of records at district/block level, discussion with workers and officials regarding implementation challenges.

In order to carry out an in-depth analysis of status and challenges involved in the implementation of scheme in the study area; discussions with participants and other stake holders such as Govt. officials were conducted for better understanding of the scheme implementation. The socio-economic context in which MGNREGS is being implemented; district administrative setup, processes and procedures were analyzed to identify the efficient management practices, procedures, processes, factors that have contributed to the good performance and factors that have resulted in limited performance. Along with secondary information on the performance of Halqa panchayat, expert interviews with block level officials particularly with the Programme Officers (PO's), Village Level Workers (VLWs) and BDOs were held in order to get an overall idea about the performance of the block as well as the halqa panchayat. At the halqa panchayat level, the information regarding MGNREGS was collected from multiple sources and stakeholders. A structured questionnaire was prepared to elicit information regarding MGNREGS from participants across sample households.

Review of Secondary Data

The review of secondary data involved first going through many research studies, articles and discussions with experts above all my supervisor. This helped in developing familiarity with implementation of MGNREGS; its procedures, processes and challenges involved. The secondary data on physical and financial performance and related information on works undertaken under MGNREGS in the state and sample districts were collected from the dedicated national web portal on MGNREGS: www.nrega.nic.in and block development office (BDO) of the concerned sample district. The present study has hugely benefited from secondary data which was collected for state, sample districts, blocks and halqa panchayats for the period between 2009-10 and 2015-16.

Primary Data

The primary data was collected at two levels; at village Level and at beneficiary level. A structured questionnaire/ schedule was developed for generating information from the beneficiary household or participant households. Before, administering the survey schedule/questionnaire in the study area, it was pre-tested for its reliability and validity, and suitably modified. The survey schedule consists of questions to extract the information regarding the socio-economic profile of the sample households working in the scheme. Besides, awareness of sample respondents about MGNREGS and their participation in works and Gram Sabhas (GSs) organised for the purpose of selection of works and social audits; details of employment sought by that household and accessed along with income gains; changing pattern of migration in the household, if any; various works or assets created in which the respondents have participated and their perception with regard to quality, durability and usefulness to community, financial integration of rural households and access to credit from formal financial institutions after MGNREGS implementation in the study area.

Data Analysis Plan

The data collected through primary and secondary sources was tabulated for analysis. All collected data and information was consolidated, cross-checked and entered in appropriate data formats. After data tabulation, the same was analysed using descriptive statistical tools such as tables, graphs, percentages, mean and cross tabulation. The hypotheses are tested using statistical tools such as One Way ANOVA, Post-hoc Test, Effect size, T-test & McNemar Test. The standard statistical software such as MS Excel and SPSS 21.0 (Statistical Package for Social Science), was used for the purpose of data analysis.

Limitations of the Study

1. The study has been undertaken in districts of Poonch and Kupwara of J&K state, which are socio-economically and geographically unique and diverse districts in the state state. It may therefore be very difficult to make generalizations to other parts of the country. However, certain characteristics of MGNREGS implemented in villages of J&K may be the same and therefore, the generalizations to other areas can be made with the limitation of the socio-economic and other characteristics of the study area.

2. The state is lagging behind in its e-governance outreach and its digitization efforts compared with the similarly situated states of north India. Therefore, the data availability via electronic sources in the context of MGNREGS in the state is limited. Besides, the studies conducted on MGNREGS either by government agencies or academic institutions in the state are few in number. So the major limitation was the non-availability of the sufficient literature concerning MGNREGS in the state.

3. The researcher has made all efforts possible to extract the correct information from the respondents, yet the peculiar behavior of some respondents might have caused limitation to some extent in extracting the correct information.

4. The operational efficacy indicators of MGNREGS have been measured subjectively using a questionnaire. Therefore, the shortcomings inherent in every questionnaire based survey where answers are dependent on respondents' perception could not be overcome. Therefore, future research works in the field need to focus on objective performance measurement wherein subjectivity has lesser effect on the validity of results.

5. Finally, the data for present study came only from the state of Jammu and Kashmir and that too from only the four blocks and halqa panchayats, Therefore, narrow geographic coverage may raise concerns about the generalization of results. It is, therefore, required that similar research may be replicated in other geographical areas covering different sectors of an economy.

Chapter II

Theoretical Foundation of Public Welfare Schemes

Theoretical and Empirical Background

The Indian Constitution, in the Directive Principles of State Policy, has emphasized that ensuring decent work for all citizens should be a crucial focus of state policy. In this context, Article 41 of the Directive Principles states that "The State shall, within the limits of its economic capacity and development, make effective provision for securing the right to work, to education and to public assistance in cases of unemployment, old age, sickness and disablement, and in other cases of underserved want". Besides, there is considerable attention given to the conditions of work and the level of wages in Articles 42 and 43, which states that "The State shall make provision for just and humane conditions of work and for maternity relief... The State shall endeavor to secure, by suitable legislation or economic organization or in any other way, to all workers, agricultural, industrial or otherwise, work at living wage, conditions of work ensuring a decent standard of life and full enjoyment of leisure and social and cultural opportunities" *(Ghosh, 2008)*. In this backdrop, Government of India launched various rural development programmes viz Community Development Programme (CDP) (1952), Small Farmers Development Agency (SFDA) (1969-70), Marginal Farmers and Agricultural Labourers (MFAL) Programme (1969-70), Integrated Rural Development Programme (IRDP) (1976-77), wage employment programmes viz. Food For Work Programme (FWP) (1977), Training For Rural Youth For Self-Employment (TRYSEM) (1979), Rural Employment Programme (1980), Jawahar Rozgar Yojana (1989), Swaranjayanti Gram Swarozgar Yojana (SGSY) (1999) & National Food For Work Programme, 2004 *(Desai, 2009)*. However, many of these programs suffered from various loopholes such as poor design and targeting, lack of active involvement of people, poor social monitoring and audit and above all, guarantee provision in these schemes was also lacking. To overcome these problems, The UPA government unanimously passed the National Rural Employment Guarantee Act (MGNREGS) in 2005. This act has been hailed as a major initiative in the Government of India's commitment to providing an economic safety net to India's rural poor. MGNREGS is the first legislation that compels the state to provide a social safety net for the poorest people of this country and seeks to address the urgent issues of hunger and rural distress that afflicts large parts of India *(Lakshman, 2007)*. As per the Planning Commission statistics, Agriculture employment growth rate of 0.40 per cent during 1993-94 to 2004-05 and that of rural non-agriculture employment growth rate of 3.52 during the same period indicates that the rural areas did not provide adequate opportunities for the population. Hence, a scheme like MGNREGS has a great potential to fill this gap *(Kareemulla et al, 2010)*. The MGNREGS has incorporated lessons from a long array of food for work programs implemented in India in the past *(Dutta et al, 2012)*. In that it features significant innovations *(Khera and Nayak, 2009)*. One such innovation is that it is designed on "self targeting" principle: the government does not determine who is poor and eligible. The self-targeting model relies on the opportunity cost of showing up to work: those who do not need the money or who can find better-paying jobs will not show up. Secondly, it establishes a legal right for households to be employed for up to 100 days per year; in fact, individuals who apply but do not receive work within a period of two weeks are entitled to unemployment allowance at minimum wages prevailing in the state *(MGNREGS, 2005-06)*. The minimum wage rate applies both to males and females, making the program particularly attractive to women, who normally receive significantly lower wages than men *(Deininger et al., 2010)*. The descriptive evidence portrays the quality of program implementation varied across states *(Liu and Barrett, 2013)* but that the program seems to have allowed households to mitigate the impacts of consumption shocks *(Coffey, Papp, and Spears, 2011)*, for example, due to variations in rainfall, and deal with large and covariant swings in asset prices *(Johnson, 2009)*. Reviews of the program found that many job seekers were unable to obtain the desired level of work, at least initially *(Dutta et al., 2012)*. Local decision makers were found to use the scheme strategically to maximize rents *(Niehaus and Sukhtankar, 2012)*. It is not too surprising to see positive program impacts on females at the descriptive level, with knock-on effects on their offspring *(Dev, 2011)*.

There are many studies which provide adequate evidence that despite a modest overall performance by the Indian economy during the past one and a half decades, the extent to which economic progress has translated into increased labour earnings consequently resulting into poverty reduction, has been rather disappointing *(Bhalla, 2002; Ghosh, 2004; Kijima and Lanjouw, 2005)*. To a large extent, this concern arises in relation to the rural workforce, which accounts to 75 per cent of the total workforce in India *(Sen and Ghosh, 1993; Nayyar, 1993; Bhalla, 1998; Sen, 1998)*. Accordingly, slow growth in labour earnings is one of the major reasons for the slower decline in poverty, particularly in the rural areas in the late 1990s and early 2000s *(Sen, 1998; Bhalla, 2002; Deaton and Dreze, 2002)*. In India, the labour market dualism has been documented widely in terms of formal-informal, employment status of workers, occupation types, sectors of employment, states and regions etc. *(Sen, 1994; Unni, 2001; Tendulkar, 2003; Das, 2003)*. Accordingly, wages and earnings of workers differ across different segments of the labour market *(Sen, 1998)*. As *Devereux (2006)* pointed out, the effect of public employment programmes on poverty reduction is directly proportional to the scale of the programme (the number and duration of jobs provided), the proportion of the budget allocated to labour costs and the level of income transferred. However, this presents policy makers with a difficult trade-off. At the household level, "tiny transfers equal tiny impacts, but moderate transfers can have major impacts" *(Devereux 2002b: 672)*. Tinbergen also observed employment guarantee programmes that made 'strategic use of surplus labour to promote economic growth in developing countries' *(Tinbergen, 1994)*. Historically speaking, public employment programmes started as relief works to provide employment and wages to people affected by disasters like droughts, floods etc. Over the years, however, they were seen as an instrument of using surplus labour for generating capital goods for increasing labour absorbing capacity of the mainstream economy *(Nurkse, 1957)*. It needs to be noted that wage employment programmes in general have come a long way from their historical origin as relief works organized for the poor in emergency situations caused by natural disasters or economic depressions and crisis. These programmes are also not seen merely as an instrument of consumption smoothing that helps the poor some support in the lean season of the year. In fact, these programmes are now recognized in the literature as a modern instrument of general development policy, as they have shown tremendous potential to alleviate poverty as part of mainstream economic strategy *(Tinbergen, 1994)*. The employment guarantee programmes will generate massive purchasing power in the economy, and this will raise the aggregate demand in the economy. Since the deficiency in the aggregate demand is a constraint to economic growth under the neoliberal policies in most developing economies, including India, employment guarantee schemes can address this deficiency adequately. In this sense a guarantee programme can give a fresh doze to revitalize the economy, *(Hirway, 2009)*. The MGNREGS, as it stands, eliminates explicitly two important criteria inherent in Employment Guarantee Schemes (EGS), particularly those that have been initiated in the State of Maharashtra: (i) public works programmes should not compete with agricultural labour hiring decisions and (ii) public works programmes should generate productive assets that directly impact agricultural productivity *(Basu et al., 2005)*.

A detailed analysis of the impact of different poverty alleviation programmes, including the wage and self employment programmes was made by *Manoj Kumar in 2007* in his book *"Political Economy of Poverty: A Micro-Level Study"*. In his study, he opined that most of the programmes aiming at poverty alleviation reflect good politics but bad economics. The book has evaluated the efficacy of the poverty alleviation programmes, self-employment programmes, wage employment programmes and national social assistance programmes on the basis of micro level study and concluded that poverty alleviation programmes have filled the coffers of a group of people who are much above the poverty line. The book also throws sufficient light on political economy of poverty besides identifying several limiting factors in way of poverty alleviation programmes. *Planning Commission (2008)* conducted a survey in 20 states to study the impact of MGNREGS. The results showed a shift of low income groups (about 50%) towards high income category, significant increase in the expenditure on food and non-food items (6%) & change in the expenditure pattern, procurement of livestock (68%) & household articles (42%). Initiation of savings for the first time (2%), clearing of outstanding loans (1/5th of sample households) were some of the positive impacts of MGNREGS on rural households. The other things they observed were the non-provision of employment within stipulated timeframe (80%) and non-payment of unemployment allowances, the utilization of small portion of households for more than 35 days of work and existence of distress migration in sample villages. *Centre for Research in Rural and Industrial Development (2009)* made an appraisal & impact assessment of NREGA programme in the sampled districts of Himachal Pradesh (Simaur), Punjab (Hoshiarpur) & Haryana (Sirsa) with the aim to find out the effective management practices, procedures & processes and also different interventions & strategies for its up scaling & dissemination. The impact assessment revealed that more than 62% of the sampled panchayats in district Sirsa & nearly 3/4th panchayats in district Simaur showed increase in their agricultural production due to the activities of MGNREGS programme. However it was also reported that more than 87% panchayats of district Hoshiarpur did not have any positive impact on agricultural production & irrigation due to MGNREGS programme. It was also observed that there was no change towards the inbound migration of the workers in the districts Simaur & Hoshiarpur where as it was reported that 37% panchayats in district sirsa observed decreased in & out migration of the villagers due to NREGA works. On the other hand it further indicated that all the panchayats of district Simaur, 3/4th panchayats of district Hoshiarpur & 50% panchayats in district Sirsa observed an overall decrease in out-migration from their villages *(CRRID, 2009)*.

Thematic Review of Literature on MGNREGS

A thematic review of some of the recent important studies relating to the performance assessment and impact of MGNREGS on livelihood of rural communities, employment generation and income, financial inclusion, rural-urban migration, awareness and participation of local communities in villages and status of assets created across the country was made.

2.2.1 Impact of MGNREGS on Asset creation, Employment, Income and Migration

Kannan, P (2005) viewed the MGNREGS as much needed developmental perspective that seeks to enhance human development by inclusion of the rural poor. He opined that the goal of investing in human capital can be completed through MGNREGS if project like construction of schools, health centres at local level along with the repairs of existing buildings. This will be the best way to utilise the unutilised potential in rural areas.

Verma (2006) he observed that unemployment is still on the increase and that the benefit of growth has failed to percolate down to the poor people especially in rural areas. He further stressed that for poverty alleviation rapid economic growth focusing mainly on labour intensive sector is required.

Dreeze and Lal (2007) based on his studies on NREGA in Rajasthan concluded that this state stands first in terms of employment generation per rural household under this scheme. They stated that in 2006-07 the average rural households in six NREGA Districts of Rajasthan got work for 77 days under this programme earning nearly Rs.4,000 in the process.

Dre'ze and Christian Oldiges (2007) based on the official data, estimated that, the employment generated under MGNREGS (90 crore person days during 2006-07) was much more than the employment generated in earlier years under NFFWP and SGRY. They also opined that the women participation in MGNREGS brings social change. The authors expressed the view that

MGNREGS has shown greater economic security and its implementation has led to rise of agricultural wages, slowing down of migration, creation of productive assets and women having more economic independence, changing power equations and so on. They concluded that the Southern state and Western states did better than most of the Northern states.

Shah. M (2008) opined that NREGA has the potential to provide "big push" to distressed sectors of Indian economy. To realize the full potential of MGNREGS the role of civil society organisations is crucial. He also opined that MGNREGS calls for a new self-critical politics of fortitude, balance and restraint.

Jacob Naomi (2008) studied the impact of NREGA on Rural-Urban migration in Villupuram district. The study observed a positive impact on employment generation, wages of participating households and increasing participation of women in the scheme. The problem areas highlighted by the study are poor awareness about scheme entitlements, faulty distribution of job cards, shortage of staff, caste segregation of work and other implementation issues need prompt policy action.

Pramathesh A, Shankar and M. Shah (2008) reported some of the lacunae in implementation of NREGA such as under staffing or lack of exclusive MGNREGS staff at lower level and top – down approach in planning of the scheme. The researchers opine that the NREGA holds the potential of positively changing the lives of rural poor and heralding a revolution in rural governance structure in India.

Ashok K Pankaj (2008) clearly indicated the relatively high share of MGNREGS income to the total income (about 8% of the total annual income of the households in Bihar and to about 2% in Jharkhand) of the beneficiary households despite the low number of employment days in Bihar (and also in Jharkhand) was because of the very low income base of the households. The beneficiaries in both the states used their MGNREGS earnings for food and daily consumption items. Due to MGNREGS a reduction of 7% indebtedness, 12 % reduction in out migration among beneficiary households was observed in Bihar. Nevertheless, it has inculcated a new level of consciousness about the entitlements such as minimum wages. An increase in the Work Participation Rate (WPR) was observed but no significant impact on the local wage because of the availability of abundance labour force and low level of employment generation under MGNREGS.

Comptroller and Auditor General of India (CAG), 2008, Published a paper on 'Performance Audit of Implementation of National Rural Employment Guarantee Act (NREGA). The request of the Ministry of Rural Development, the CAG undertook an audit in 2006 to evaluate how effectively states were making a transition from the earlier wage employment programmes to the MGNREGS. The audit was conducted in 26 states and the sample for the audit included 25 per cent of the MGNREGS districts in each state. The audit was conducted in the introductory phase of the Act and a majority of the findings of the audit were process deviations with regard to the National Guidelines. It is important to note that several states took action on the findings of the CAG and introduced systems to prevent procedural deviations and promote transparency in the implementation of the scheme.

Ghosh, J (2008) wrote in an article, that MGNREGS is actually far from being an expensive failure. The scheme will prove to be an extremely cost-effective way of increasing employment directly and indirectly reviving the rural economy, providing basic consumption stability to poor households and improving the bargaining power of rural workers. The argument is well supported by various other studies on the subject.

Planning Commission (2008) conducted a survey in 20 states to study the impact of MGNREGS. The results showed a shift of low income groups (about 50%) towards high income category, significant increase in the expenditure on food and non-food items (6%) and change in the expenditure pattern, procurement of livestock (68%) and household articles (42%) and initiation of savings for the first time (2%), clearing of outstanding loans (1/5th of sample households) were some of the positive impacts of MGNREGS on rural households. The other things that were ported include the non-provision of employment within stipulated timeframe (80%) and non-payment of unemployment allowances, the utilization of small portion of households for more than 35 days of work and existence of distress migration in sample villages.

Indian Institute of Management Shillong (2009) studied the implementation of MGNREGS in six districts has indicated that MGNREGS has sufficiently added to household income of the people who have worked/working in MGNREGS. The workers were of opinion that they have been able to support their households' daily food requirements.

Dutta, S K (2009) carried a quick appraisal of MGNREGS in Dangs (Gujarat) and Jalpaiguri (West Bengal) districts and reported that the mobility and interactions of community increased to due to the impact of rural connectivity works. Migrations also become limited to only one member of a family during slack season due to availability of work locally. The report also indicates that even though people are not well aware of works carried out in their village under MGNREGS, improvement in water availability has been observed by them. Further, hardly any permanent assets have been created out of NREGS fund due the stipulated norm of 60:40 ratio between labour and material cost and also due to lack of coordination with line departments.

Singh S P and D K Nauriyal (2009) assessed the impact of MGNREGS in three districts of Uttarakhand and reported that NREGS activities were found to be supplementing income of the household to the extent of 10-20 per cent and hence no significant improvement in their income and employment levels. Further, marginal improvement in curtail of migration and indebtedness were found. Increase in consumption levels and savings were also marginally improved among the sample households. The report indicates that lack of procedures, low levels of awareness and weak PRIs etc., were the reasons for low performance of MGNREGS in the sample districts.

Johson, D (2009) observed that MGNREGS doesn't just provide money to poor households but it provides money when they most need it. He suggested that if households are able to use MGNREGS as an ex-post substitute for formal weather insurance, then they may be able to shift away from investments in low-risk, low-return assets to higher-risk and higher-return assets.

Jha et al. (2009) observed that landholding of a household is a negative predictor of employment provided under MGNREGS in Rajasthan. However, the relationship turns positive in Andhra Pradesh as households with larger landholdings show a substantial participation in the scheme. The difference arises due to varied level of land distribution in the two states (more inequality in AP than in Rajasthan) and higher ratio of MGNREGS wage to agricultural wage rates.

Sainath, P (2009) asked in his article for expansion of MGNREGS, universal access to the PDS, more spending on health and education. He commented that a positive step taken by the Rural

Development Ministry. It allows small but vital assets like farm ponds on every farm which should become the objective of every government. A massive expansion of MGNREGS will also provide cushion to the lakhs of labourers struggling to find work and devastated by rising food costs. But it would call for throwing out the limit on number days of work under the scheme. He explained that the Prime Minister calling for anti drought measures on "a war footing" and this should be the time to do it.

Swaminathan, M S (2009) highlighted that the priority works under MGNREGS are important to strengthen the ecological foundations of sustainable agriculture. He also commented that a major weakness was the absence of effective technical guidance and support from agriculture and rural universities and institutes. He suggested the need to bring convergence of child care, nutritional health and education programmes at MGNREGS worksites for sustainable rural development along with human development. He opined that the MGNREGS workers need to be engaged in checking of eco-destruction. Recognition could be given to MGNREGS workers with Environment Savior Awards for their outstanding work for sustainable ecological development.

Chapter III

Financial Inclusion & Analysis

Financial Inclusion Under Mahatma Gandhi National Rural Employment Guarantee Scheme (MGNREGS).

Financial inclusion may be defined as the process of ensuring access to financial services, timely and adequate credit availability for low income and backward sections of the society at an affordable cost *(Ministry of Finance, 2008)*. The access to financial services includes access to banks/post office accounts, payment & remittances, affordable credit/loans, insurance (health & property) and financial advice etc. Financial inclusion in an open market economy is empirically recognized as being not only pro-growth but also pro-poor, thus enabling reduction in poverty and income inequality *(Asian Development Bank, 2011)*.

Legislative measures have been introduced in various countries to push an inclusive financial system for instance in The Community Reinvestment Act (1977) in United States of America requires banks to provide credit to all families in their neighborhood prohibiting them in specifically targeting the wealthy neighborhoods only. Similarly, in France, the Law of Exclusion emphasizes an individual's right to have a bank account and in U.K , a 'Financial Inclusion Task Force' was constituted by the government in 2005 in order to monitor the progress the on financial inclusion *(Sarma, et al., 2011)*. In India, the Reserve Bank of India (RBI) has initiated several measures to achieve greater financial inclusion such as facilitating 'no-frills' accounts and 'General Credit Cards' for low deposit and credit such as Zero Balance Accounts, Kisan Credit Cards (KCC), Soil Cards, Artisan Credit Cards.

The lack of financial inclusion is a global problem but in India it has assumed staggering scale considering only 55% of Indian population have bank accounts and only 9% have credit accounts. There is only around 20% of life insurance penetration and less than 10% of property/ non-life insurance penetration in India, only 18% have debit cards & less than 2% have credit cards, which indicates that financial exclusion is a massive problem in India *(Chakrabarty, 2011)*.

In emerging economies such as India with staggering financial exclusion the access to financial services such as bank/post office account, access to affordable credit/loan, direct transfer of wages and remittances, insurance etc. more than the knowledge about transparency and fairness of these financial services is of considerable importance for making a transition towards a financially inclusive economy. Therefore, the key role of Mahatma Gandhi National Rural Employment Guarantee Scheme (MGNREGS) in financial inclusion has also been acknowledged by The Rangarajan Committee on Financial Inclusion *(Ministry of Finance, 2008)*. The importance of MGNREGS becomes even more vital given majority of rural population (80%) are either landless or marginal landholding farmers, who rarely have work on their own farms for more than 100 days a year. Hence, the availability of guaranteed wage employment increases the prospects of a financially inclusive rural sector *(Jain, et al. 2013)*.

An inclusive financial system has three dimensions namely accessibility, availability and usage of banking services *(Sarma, 2011)*. The present study has endeavored to explore the impact of MGNREGS on financial inclusion measured by the number of bank/post office accounts opened post scheme implementation (secondary data), frequency of account usage pattern, purpose for which the bank or post-office account is operated by beneficiary households, improvement in access to bank credit after MGNREGS implementation in the study area (primary data).

Status of Financial Inclusion in The Study Area Under MGNREGS

Table 10.6 & fig. 4.2 depicts the overall active accounts in various banks and post offices in Kupwara & Poonch district of J&K state. A total of 15,41,525 MGNREGS accounts are active in J&K state in the year 2016-17, out of which 1,27,404 accounts have been generated in district Kupwara & 1,11,426 in Poonch district. The number of MGNREGS accounts generated through post offices is much lower as compared to bank accounts at both district and state level, which is quite natural due to low penetration and banking being the peripheral activity of the post offices. The funds flow through bank and postal accounts was Rs 2448 (twenty four hundred and forty eight lakhs) in district Kupwara and Rs 2900 (twenty nine hundred lakh) in Poonch district whereas Rs 37025 lakh was distributed through bank and postal accounts of the MGNREGS beneficiaries in J&K state. The distribution of wages through accounts brings transparency, accountability and protects corruption in the system of wage and material expenditure delivery. It also helps in controlling the duplicate and ghost workers in the system with help of Aadhar Biometric identification, which has now been made mandatory for delivery of social and other benefits in India.

There was 100% financial inclusion as for as the participating rural workers/households in MGNREGS in the study area is concerned which was also verified by the survey data from the sample beneficiaries. There was 100% distribution of wages through the bank and postal accounts in sample districts that is a great achievement for deeper financial inclusion of the rural communities.

Table 10.6: Status of Active MGNREGS Accounts in Kupwara, Poonch & J&K State

Region	No. of Banks Accounts	No. of Post office Accounts	Total Wage Amount Disbursed (in Lakhs)
Kupwara	127357	47	2448
Poonch	109926	1500	2900
J&K State	1532726	8799	37025

Source: *www.nrega.nic.in accessed on 08/04/2017*

Figure 4.2: Status of Bank Accounts in Sample Districts & J&K State

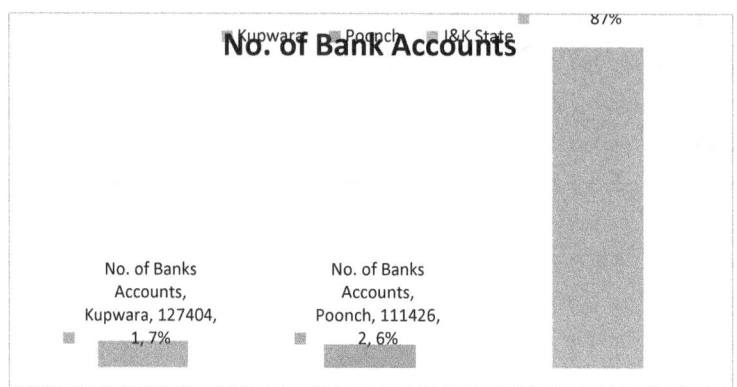

The block wise number of MGNREGS bank and post office accounts is depicted in table 10.7 & fig. 4.3. Two thousand five hundred and nine accounts are generated under MGNREGS in Langate block as compared to five thousand one hundred and sixty bank accounts in Trehgam block of district Kupwara. Similarly, twelve thousand eight hundred and seven MGNREGS bank accounts have been opened in block Surankote which is almost equal to 12800 bank accounts opened in block Poonch under the scheme. The number of bank accounts generated in MGNREGS in the study area is quite staggering considering the small population of these areas. The flow of wages under MGNREGS scheme through bank accounts was Rs 627.84 lakhs which is quite a big number and would deepen the financial inclusion efforts by all the organized financial institutions such as commercial, RRB's and Cooperative banks in the study area and in other areas also as the massive funds flow incentivizes the efforts of banks to push the financial integration of unbanked or under banked areas.

Table 10.7: Block Wise Status of Active MGNREGS Accounts in Banks & Post Offices

Districts	Blocks	No. of Banks Accounts	No. of Post office Accounts	Total Wage Amount Disbursed (in Lakhs)
	Langate	2509	0	63.12

Kupwara	Trehgam	5160	0	33.26
Poonch	Surankote	12807	0	302.19
	Poonch	12800	0	229.27
	Total	33276	0	627.84

Source: www.nrega.nic.in accessed on 08/04/2017

Figure 4.3: Block Wise Status of Bank Accounts Under MGNREGS

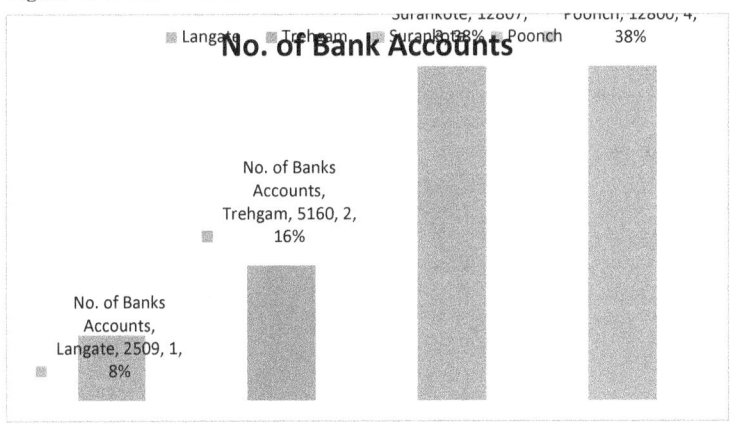

4.6.2 Respondents' Frequency of Bank Account Usage

The frequency of bank account usage depicts how much the beneficiary is actively using the banking services. The frequency of account usage is measured Once, Twice and more than Thrice a month. Table 10.8 & fig. 4.4 shows that 42.50% respondents use bank account more than thrice a month, 32% respondents use the bank account twice a month and remaining 25.50% respondents use it only once a month. This indicates that despite all the geographic and institutional delivery constraints the target population has responded positively to the new found financial experience. The survey data also revealed that 100% financial inclusion was achieved under MGNREGS for the sample respondents only after working in MGNREGS. It is quite clear that the impact on financial inclusion is positive and has the potential to further deepen this process under the scheme in the study area.

Table 10.8: Frequency of Bank Account Usage

Frequency of Bank Account Usage (Monthly)	Frequency	Percent
ONCE	51	25.50
TWICE	64	32
MORE THAN TWICE	85	42.50
Total	200	100.0

Source: Survey Data

Figure 4.4: Frequency of Bank Account Usage Under MGNREGS

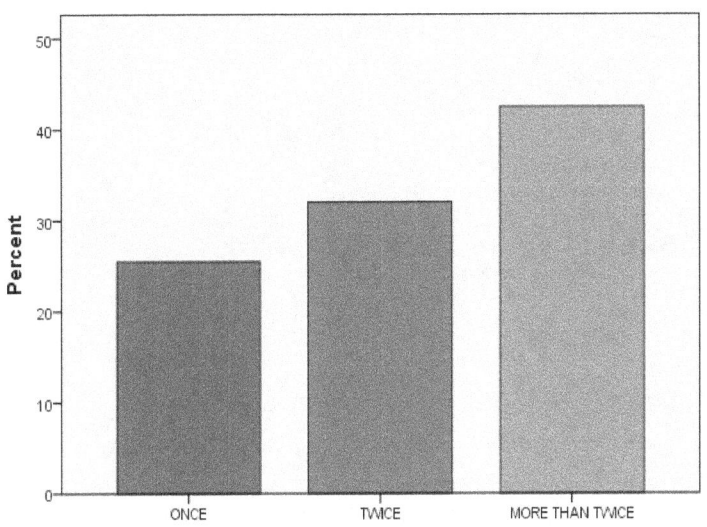

Frequency of Bank Account Usage

4.6.3 Respondents' Bank Account Usage Pattern in MGNREGS

The data on usage pattern of bank account is presented in table 10.9 & fig. 4.5. Respondents' were asked about why they use or operate a bank account?. Table 10.8 depicts that 90% respondents reported that they use a bank account for saving money, 100% respondents reported that the bank account is used for receiving wages under MGNREGS, only 27% reported transferring money as one of the purpose for operating a bank account, 91.50% reported for receiving various social benefits such as subsidy on various public goods such as gas, rice etc. whereas just 6% reported other use for operating a bank account.

Table 10.9: Respondent's Usage Pattern of Bank Account in MGNREGS

Bank Account Usage Pattern	Frequency	Percent
Savings	180	90%

Receiving Wages	200	100%
Transferring Money	54	27%
Receiving Subsidy	183	91.50%
Other Uses	12	6%

Source: Survey Data

Figure 4.5: Bank Account Usage Pattern in MGNREGS

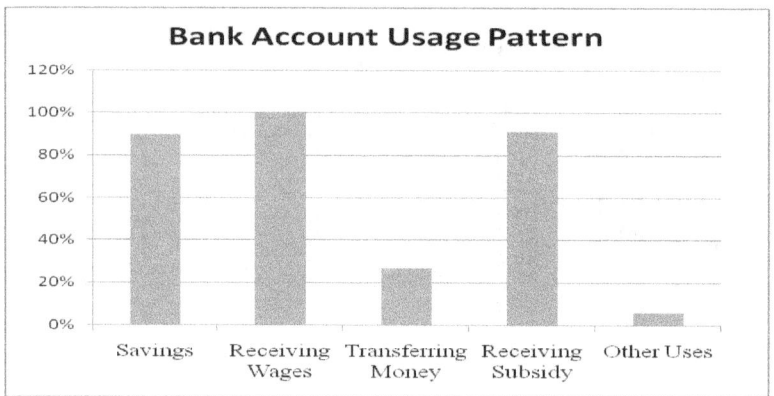

In order to verify whether there is any difference in access to bank credit post MGNREGS implementation across income status, land ownership, social group and gender. The present study hypothesizes that access to bank credit across socio-economic status is same after the scheme was implemented in the study area. The analysis was done on perceptual data extracted from the beneficiary households with the help of a survey instrument.

Null Hypothesis:

H04: There is no significant difference in access to bank credit Post MGNREGS implementation across socio-economic status of rural households.

H04a: There is no significant difference in access to bank credit Post MGNREGS implementation between APL, BPL & AAY households.

H04b: There is no significant difference in access to bank credit Post MGNREGS implementation between Marginal Farmers (MF), Small Farmers (SF) & Landless Labourers (LL).

H04c: There is no significant difference in access to bank credit Post MGNREGS implementation between SC, ST, OBC & GEN Category households.

H04d: There is no significant difference in access to bank credit Post MGNREGS implementation between Male & Female beneficiaries.

Dependent Variable: Access to Bank Credit   *Independent Variable:* Socio-economic Status

Null Hypothesis:

H04a: There is no significant difference in access to bank credit Post MGNREGS implementation between APL, BPL & AAY households.

Table 11.0 depicts that the access to bank credit Post MGNREGS implementation between rural households based on income status has remained same with slight variation in mean scores. The mean scores for access to bank credit for APL respondents is 1.38, the mean score for BPL respondents is 1.35 and 1.29 for poorest of the poor (AAY) rural households. It implies that MGNREGS has had no influence on access to bank credit for the target group. The means scores are tested for statistical significance using One Way ANOVA.

Table 11.0: Mean & Std. Deviation Scores on Access to Bank Credit After MGNREGS Implementation

Income Status	N	Mean	Std. Deviation

APL	84	1.38	.558
BPL	88	1.35	.548
AAY	28	1.29	.535
Total	200	1.36	.548

Source: Survey Data

The homogeneity of variances was not significant, p =.589 > α .05. This is indicated by the Levene's Test of Homogeneity of Variances, $F(2, 197) = .530$, p=.589 with an alpha level of .05. Therefore, One Way ANOVA was applied after satisfying the assumption of equality of variances.

Table 11.1: Test of Homogeneity of Variances

Levene Statistic	df1	df2	Sig.
.530	2	197	.589

A One Way Analysis of Variance (ANOVA) test was conducted to verify the statistical significance of the difference in average scores in access to bank credit between beneficiary households across income status. The participant workers were divided into three groups; APL households, BPL households & AAY households. There was no statistically significant difference in average scores in access to bank credit for these three groups with $F(2, 197) = .317, p = .729$.

Based on ANOVA F ratio results the null hypothesis is accepted and alternative hypothesis is rejected.

Table 11.2: One Way ANOVA Between Income Status & Access to Bank Credit

	Sum of Squares	df	Mean Square	F	Sig.
Between Groups	.192	2	.096	.317	.729
Within Groups	59.603	197	.303		
Total	59.795	199			

Null Hypothesis:

H04b: There is no significant difference in access to bank credit Post MGNREGS implementation between Marginal Farmers (MF), Small Farmers (SF) & Landless Labourers (LL).

The data on access to bank credit after MGNREGS implementation is reported below in table 11.3. The access to bank credit average score for marginal farmers (MF) is 1.37 (SD=.575), 1.40 (SD=.516) for small farmers & 1.34 (SD=.540) average score for landless labourers (LL). The difference in mean scores between these three groups is small and was tested for statistical significance for difference in mean scores using One Way ANOVA.

Table 11.3: Mean & Std. Deviation Scores on Access to Bank Credit Across Land Ownership Status

Land Ownership Status	N	Mean	Std. Deviation
Marginal Farmers (MF)	65	1.37	.575
Small Farmers (SF)	10	1.40	.516
Landless Labourers (LL)	125	1.34	.540
Total	200	1.36	.548

Source: Survey Data

The homogeneity of variances was not significant, $p = .882 > \alpha\ .05$. This is indicated by the Levene's Test of Homogeneity of Variances, $F (2, 197) = .125$, $p=.882$ with an alpha level of .05. Therefore, One Way ANOVA was applied after satisfying the assumption of equality of variances.

Table 11.4: Test of Homogeneity of Variances

Levene Statistic	df1	df2	Sig.
.125	2	197	.882

One Way Analysis of Variance (ANOVA) test was conducted to verify the statistical significance of the difference in average scores in access to bank credit between beneficiary households across Land Ownership status. The participant workers were divided into three groups; Marginal Farmers(MF), Small Farmers (SF) & Landless Labourers (LL). There was no statistically significant difference in average scores in access to bank credit for these three groups with $F(2, 197) = .080, p = .923$

The hypothesis that there is no significant difference in access to bank credit between Marginal Farmers, Small Farmers and Landless Labourers after MGNREGS implementation is accepted and alternative hypothesis is rejected.

Table 11.5: One Way ANOVA Between Land Ownership Status & Access to Bank Credit

	Sum of Squares	df	Mean Square	F	Sig.
Between Groups	.049	2	.024	.080	.923
Within Groups	59.746	197	.303		
Total	59.795	199			

Null Hypothesis:

H04c: There is no significant difference in access to bank credit Post MGNREGS implementation between SC, ST, OBC & GEN Category households.

The data on access to bank credit after MGNREGS implementation between various social groups is reported below in table 11.6. The access to bank credit average score for marginal SC Households is 1.17 (SD=.408), 1.42 (SD=.564) for ST Households, 1.27 (SD=.452) OBC Households and average score for GEN Social Group is 1.36 (SD=.567). The difference in mean scores between these four social groups is small and was tested for statistical significance for difference in mean scores using One Way ANOVA.

Table 11.6: Descriptive Score on Access to Bank Credit Between Various Social Groups

Social Groups	N	Mean	Std. Deviation
SC	6	1.17	.408
ST	31	1.42	.564
OBC	26	1.27	.452
GEN	137	1.36	.567
Total	200	1.36	.548

Source: Survey Data

The homogeneity of variances was not significant, p =.100> α .05. This is indicated by the Levene's Test of Homogeneity of Variances, $F(3, 196) = 2.110$, p=.100 with an alpha level of .05. Therefore, One Way ANOVA was applied after satisfying the assumption of equality of variances.

Table 11.7: Test of Homogeneity of Variances

Levene Statistic	df1	df2	Sig.
2.110	3	196	.100

One Way Analysis of Variance (ANOVA) test was conducted to verify the statistical significance of the difference in average scores in access to bank credit between various social groups. The participant workers were divided into four groups; SC, ST, OBC & GEN Category Social Group. There was no statistically significant difference in average scores in access to bank credit for these four groups with $F(2, 196) = .602, p = .614$

The hypothesis that there is no significant difference in access to bank credit between SC, ST, OBC & GEN Category households after MGNREGS implementation is accepted and alternative hypothesis is rejected.

Table 11.8: One Way ANOVA Between Social Groups & Access to Bank Credit

	Sum of Squares	df	Mean Square	F	Sig.
Between Groups	.546	3	.182	.602	.614

Within Groups	59.249	196	.302		
Total	59.795	199			

Null Hypothesis:

H04d: There is no significant difference in access to bank credit Post MGNREGS implementation between Male & Female beneficiaries.

The average and Std. deviation scores for access to bank credit post MGNREGS implementation between Male & Female Workers is reported below in table 11.9. The access to bank credit mean score for Male workers is 1.34 (SD=.561) and Female workers is 1.41 (SD=.499). The difference in mean scores between male and female MGNREGS beneficiaries is small which was test for statistical significance using Independent Samples t-test.

Table 11.9: Access to Bank Credit Score Between Male & Female MGNREGS Workers

Gender	N	Mean	Std. Deviation
MALE	159	1.34	.561
FEMALE	41	1.41	.499

Source: Survey Data

The assumption of homogeneity of variances was verified before conducting independent samples t-test. The variances in average Scores for Access to Bank Credit between Male & Female MGNREGS Workers was same with p= .747.

An independent samples t-test was conducted to compare the mean difference in access to bank credit after MGNREGS implementation between Male & Female Workers. There was no significant difference in the scores for access to bank credit between *Male Workers (M*=1.34, *SD=.561) and Female Workers (M=*1.41, *SD=.499); t (198)* = -.780, *p* = .436.

		Levene's Test for Equality of Variances		t-test for Equality of Means						
		F	Sig.	t	df	Sig.(2-tailed)	MD	Std. Error Difference	95% C I of the Difference	
									Lower	Upper
Access to Bank Credit	Equal variances assumed	.105	.747	-.780	198	.436	-.075	.096	-.265	.115
	Equal variances not assumed			-.836	68.468	.406	-.075	.090	-.254	.104

Table 12.0: Independent Sample t-Test

4.7 MGNREGS and Migration

The present study has endeavored to understand the impact of Mahatma Gandhi National Rural Employment Guarantee Scheme (MGNREGS) on migration in the study area. The study further investigated into the reasons behind migration Post-MGNREGS implementation. The hypothesis testing was conducted using non-parametric McNemar's Test for determining the statistical significance of the impact of MGNREGS.

Chapter IV

Conclusion

The present research study was carried out with a broad objective to evaluate the operational efficacy of Mahatma Gandhi National Rural Employment Guarantee Scheme by utilizing both the primary and secondary data. The researcher attempted to achieve this objective by examining the impact on employment (Average Man-days) and addition to household income, income consumption pattern under the scheme, awareness and participation, impact on financial inclusion, impact on labour migration Post-MGNREGS and impact on asset creation in the scheme.

The present study has endeavored to test the hypotheses related to influence of socio-economic status of rural households on participation (employment) and income, financial inclusion, perception towards various tangible assets created under MGNREGS and labour migration (Post MGNREGS). The researcher also looked into various issues and challenges involved in the effective implementation of the scheme by relying on both primary and data. The various findings from the study have been summarized as under:

5.2 Findings from Secondary Source

Mahatma Gandhi National Rural Employment Guarantee Scheme (MGNREGS) has made significant achievements in providing gainful employment to socially and economically disadvantaged groups such as BPL households, SC's, ST's, OBC's and women. It has generated sustainable assets in agriculture sector at a massive scale and has generated more employment for rural poor than any other social protection scheme in the history of India.

Persondays Generated: The persondays generated in the state of J&K under the scheme has gone down from 3.65 crore in FY 2012-13 to 3.16 crore in FY 2015-16. The persondays generated in district Kupwara has gone up from 20.32 lakh in FY 2012-13 to 21.12 lakh in FY 2015-16 which is a significant improvement over three year period given the higher wages in other sectors. The performance in persondays generated in district Poonch has significantly gone down from 28.06 lakh in FY 2012-13 to 21.90 lakh in FY 2015-16.

Share of SCs, STs & Women in Persondays: The national level participation of SCs has gone down from 29% in FY 2008-09 to 22.40% in FY 2014-15, similarly, the participation of STs has also significantly declined from 25% in FY 2008-09 to 16.97% in FY 2014-15. However, the percentage share of women workers in overall persondays generated has consistently moved upwards from 48% in FY 2008-09 to 54.88% in FY 2014-15. This is a remarkable achievement for inclusion of women in the labour market. The percentage of SC, ST & Women participation in persondays generated in the state was 5.83%, 16.81% & 25.28% respectively in FY 2015-16. The state figures for inclusion of socially disadvantaged groups is positive and better than the national figures.

Average Days of Employment Per Household: The average number of employment days provided to participating households has been increasing from year to year till 2009-10 as it reached 54 days. However, it has gone down to 40 days in 2014-15 which is significantly lower than the guaranteed 100 days in MGNREGA Act (2005-06). The average number of employment days per household in J&K has gone down from 56.54 in FY 2012-13 to 48.54 in FY 2015-16. The average days of employment per household has gone down from 55.38 in FY 2012-13 to 48.53 in FY 2015-16 for Kupwara and from 67.70 in FY 2012-13 to 55.83 in FY 2015-16 for district Poonch. The data on average persondays for every participating household in the scheme is abject and poor both for state of J&K and at All India level.

Households Completed 100 days in MGNREGS: The total number of households who have completed 100 days of wage employment in MGNREGS in J&K has gone down by more than 50% from 69,381 in FY 2012-13 to 34,675 in FY 2015-16 that too in just three years. The 100 days wage employment target was also far below the guaranteed 100 days in all the four blocks and was hovering around on an average 40-50 days per households in each block.

Household with Job Cards: The total number of issued job cards in the state was around 12.95 lakh in FY 2016-17 and the number of active job cards was only 9.38 lakhs with a deficit of over 2 lakh job cards. The percentage of SC & ST workers against active workers was over 19% in FY 2016-17 in the state. The problem of lack of active job cards has to do with the lack of ground staff at the village and block level as the awareness is high among the rural households as was observed by the survey.

Total Expenditure, Wage Expenditure, and Wages Liability: The total expenditure in MGNREGS at the National Level has gone down from Rs 27,250 crore in FY 2008-09 to Rs 24,800 crore in FY 2014-15 i.e. around 10% decline in overall expenditure in six year period. The expenditure on unskilled wages has also gone down from Rs 18200 in FY 2008-09 to Rs 16368 in FY 2014-15 which is 66% of total expenditure.

The percentage utilization of available funds in the state was at a staggering rate of 97.24% in FY 2015-16. However, the total expenditure in the state under the scheme has gone down from Rs 85,334 Lakhs in FY 2012-13 to Rs 76,853.05 Lakhs in FY 2015-16. The wage liability under MGNREGS has gone up from Rs 1.43 crore in FY 2012-13 to Rs 99.36 crore in FY 2015-16. The wage liability is primarily due to delayed payments and it is not due to unavailability of the funds in the scheme. Another problem is very high percentage of expenditure of around 59% on material and administrative component of the scheme and only 41% was spent on wages for unskilled, semi-skilled and skilled workers in the scheme in FY 2015-16.

Asset Creation: The creation of durable & productive assets in rural agrarian economy is the most fundamental objectives of the scheme. The works on irrigation canals, drainage, water conservation, and laying of other social infrastructure such as drinking water, school infrastructure, link roads etc. are some of the major works under taken in the state of J&K. The total number of works taken up for execution in the state has gone up from 1.48 lakh in FY 2012-13 to 1.88 lakh in FY 2015-16. However, the work completion rate is very poor in the state as the number of works completed in FY 2012-13 was only 57,691 out of 1.48 lakh works taken up for execution which is only 38% work completion percentage for the same period. Similarly, the completed works was only 84,226 out of 1.88 lakh for FY 2015-16. The expenditure on works related to agriculture and allied activities has risen from 41.68% in FY 2012-13 to 45.10% in FY 2015-16. The works completed in district Kupwara in FY 2015-16 was only around 10,000 out of 17,000 works taken up for execution in the district. Similarly, in Poonch district the works completed for FY 2015-16 was only around 8000 out of 20,000 works taken up for execution in the district. The percentage of expenditure on agriculture related works in the Poonch has gone down from 54.26% in FY 2012-13 to 51.60% in FY 2015-16.

Financial Inclusion (Bank & Post Office Accounts): A total of 15,41,525 MGNREGS accounts are active in J&K state under MGNREGS in the year 2016-17, out of which 1,27,404 accounts have been generated in district Kupwara & 1,11,426 in Poonch district. The funds flow through bank and postal accounts was Rs 2448 (twenty four hundred and forty eight lakhs) in district Kupwara and Rs 2900 (twenty nine hundred lakh) in Poonch district whereas Rs 37025 lakh was distributed through bank and postal accounts of the MGNREGS beneficiaries in J&K state. The disbursal of funds through accounts of beneficiaries reduces the chances of corruption and enhances the penetration of formal banking among rural communities.

5.3 Findings from Primary Source

Social Audit: The MGNREGA Act (2005-06) provides for social audit to be held after every six months but in the study area no social audit was held & even majority of the people were not aware of social audit. This is a major challenge for implementing agencies to ensure that the regular audits are conducted as the positive impact of the scheme is heavily dependent on the accountability of implementing agencies through the instrument of social audit. Around 40% of respondents reported that social audit was never conducted in their block and 49% respondents reported that social audit was rarely conducted. It partially explains as to why the scheme has been poorly implemented in the study area as panchayat and block level officials don't conduct social audits.

Work Contracts: The MGNREGA Act (2005-06) prohibits contracting various works in the scheme as it aims to eliminate the system of middlemen for better delivery of benefits to the rural communities. However, it was observed during field discussions with villagers and other officials that work contracts are provided under the scheme to people who are close to higher ups and political parties. The wage component is then transferred to the accounts of bogus workers which are paid a small amount to maintain silence while the corrupt practice goes on. However, some field officials reported inability in engaging people at meager wage rate in the scheme which forces them to engage in work contracting in the scheme.

Awareness on Entitlements under the Act/Scheme: The reported awareness about job card being a right in the scheme was 100%, 77.50% respondents reported that they are aware about work within 15 days deadline and 53.50% respondents reported awareness about right to get unemployment allowance if work was not provided within 15 days. However, in the study area none of the workers have received unemployment allowance. It is interesting to mention that there is a significant decline in awareness scores about work within 15 days and unemployment allowance if work was not provided within 15 days from 77.50% to 53.50% i.e. a 24% drop in awareness level about two sides of the same right in the scheme. The effective delivery of scheme benefits can't be achieved without the target populations' complete information about various entitlements in the scheme.

About 15% respondents reported awareness about travel allowance if work was provided beyond 5 KMs distance from home and 15% respondents reported that they were aware about minimum wage rate prevailing in the state. Once again the level of awareness about these two entitlements is poor which may be due to lack of effort on the part of lower level implementing actors such as block level officers, panchayat institutions and lack of gram sabhas in educating poor rural households about various rights in the scheme. The awareness about 33% reservation for women and worksite facilities (such as toilets, drinking water, emergency health care etc.) in MGNREGS was only 62.50% & 63.50% respectively. The awareness level on 100 days job guarantee in a year was about 96.50% that is quite significant given poor awareness level about the scheme. The present study has tried to understand the medium of awareness for better implementation of the scheme in the study area. The respondents reported Panchayat office (79.50%) and MGNREGS Workers (89%) as a major source of information about the scheme. The combined percentage of T.V & News Papers as a medium of information about MGNREGS was only 12.50% across all the sample blocks in the study area. The respondents reported Radio as third major source of information about the scheme which is about 44% of total respondents. The low score on print and electronic media as a source of information about the scheme reflects the poor implementation of the scheme in the study area which badly affects the delivery of benefits to the target population. The poor participation as evident from low average man-days generation may be due to lack of information, education and communication efforts of the implementing machinery.

Impact on Employment (Man-days generated): The total man-days worked by the beneficiary respondents are 11527 and overall average man-days generated is only 57 against the guaranteed 100 days in a year. It is quite evident that the overall impact on employment generation in all sample blocks is poor as can been seen from the low average man-days figures. The average man-days generated in Surankote & Langate blocks are 67 and 51 man-days respectively whereas the average Man-days generated is 56 and 57 for block Poonch & Trehgam respectively. Therefore, the impact on employment generation in Surankote and Trehgam is better than other two blocks in the study area.

Average Man-days for SC, ST, OBC & Women Workers: The average man-days worked by SC, ST & OBC rural households is 84, 74, 54 man-days respectively. The participation of backward communities such as SCs & STs in terms of number of man-days is different & considerably higher than the Gen. category households which shows that the impact on these communities is much better than socially upward communities. The average days of employment for women workers is 63 days which is much higher than male workers of 56 days in the study area.

Average Man-days for AAY & BPL Households: The participation of low income households such as AAY (poorest of the poor) & BPL (Poor) in MGNREGS is much better than the APL (relatively good income) households with 70, 68 & 43 man-days respectively. It reveals better impact of the scheme on economically weaker sections of the rural communities.

Participation of Landless Labourers: The average(mean) man-days for marginal farmers was 50 days in a year, 46 man-days for small farmers and the highest number of man-days participation was by landless labourers. Therefore, the higher participation in MGNREGS by economically backward rural households indicates postive impact on these communities.

Impact on Household Income: The data on total and average addition to household income as reported by respondents in block Trehgam was Rs 426,300 and Rs 8,526 respectively. Whereas, for block Langate, Poonch and Surankote the average addition to household income from MGNREGS was Rs 7,526, Rs 8,415 & Rs 10,017 respectively. It is quite evident from data that the highest average wage earning was reported in block Surankote.

Impact on Incomes of SCs, STs, OBCs & Women Workers: The average wage earning by SC workers was Rs 12650 & ST workers was Rs 11075 which was highest by any social group among the respondents. The average wage earnings by GEN. category participating households was Rs 8645 which was lowest among the respondents. The average wages earned by Female workers in the scheme was Rs 8,442 which is lower than the average wages earned by Male workers of Rs 9,435. The deviation in average wages could be attributed to lesser participation by female workers in the scheme in the sample blocks.

Average Addition to Household Income of Landless Labourers: The average wages earned by landless laborers is Rs 9,404 which is higher than marginal and small farmers' average wage earnings of Rs 7,450 and Rs 6,945 respectively. It is quite pertinent that the most vulnerable section of the rural economy; the landless laborers who rely heavily on daily wages and have no other alternative source of income benefit most from the MGNREGS in the study area. This once again highlights the relevance of the scheme for the most deprived segment of the rural sector, continuation and increasing the minimum daily wage component would go a long way in enhancing their quality of life.

Income Consumption Pattern of MGNREGS Beneficiary Households: All the respondents in sample blocks i.e. 100% reported that they spent the income from MGNREGS on food items whereas the income spent on education of children in all sample blocks is about 99% with slight inter-block deviation of expenditure pattern on education. The overall expenditure on medicine is 88% whereas only 14.50% reported expenditure on leisure activities. Besides, the income utilized on repayment of debt by respondent households is moderate 52% & expenditure on other uses is only 10%. The respondents reported that the scheme has enabled them to spend income on non-food items such as debt repayment, education of children and medicine for the first time in their lives.

Perception of Rural Households on the Quality, Durability and Usability(Relevance) of Assets in MGNREGS: The rural communities evualuation of various assets in the scheme is very high and positive on quality, durability and usability dimensions. However, in the present we have tried to see whether the perception scores vary across socio-economic status of respondents and it was observed that the positive evaluation comes from socially and economically better of communities in the rural kashmir. It was due to low relevance of assets for the socially and economically weaker sections of the rural hinterland in the study area.

Frequency and Usage Pattern of Banks/Post office Accounts: The frequency of bank account usage depicts how much the beneficiary is actively using the banking services. It was observed that 42.50% respondents use bank account more than thrice a month, 32% respondents use the bank account twice a month and remaining 25.50% respondents use it only once a month. This indicates that despite all the geographic and institutional delivery constraints the target population has responded positively to the new found financial experience. The survey data also revealed that 100% financial inclusion was achieved under MGNREGS for the sample respondents only after working in MGNREGS. It is quite clear that the impact on financial inclusion is positive and has the potential to further deepen this process under the scheme in the study area.

It was further observed that 90% respondents reported that they use a bank account for saving money, 100% respondents reported that the bank account is used for receiving wages under MGNREGS, only 27% reported transferring money as one of the purpose for operating a bank account, 91.50% reported for receiving various social benefits such as subsidy on various public goods such as gas, rice etc. whereas just 6% reported other use for operating a bank account.

Impact on Labour Migration: All the respondents i.e. 100% reported that they migrated to work in other districts before MGNREGS was implemented in their villages. However, after the scheme was implemented the migration percentage was down to 80.50% in the study area. Post-MGNREGS implementation around 39 rural households decided not migrate for work to other districts or states. It indicates that there is a positive impact on rural labour migration in the study area.

Reasons for Migration: The respondents who migrated post MGNREGS implementation in the study area, 96.27% reported low wages or (higher wages outside of MGNREGS) as one of the reasons for migration, 95.65% reported limited work days, 74.53% reported delayed work after the application for work was made as one of the reasons for migration, 75.15% respondents reported delayed wages as the basic reason for migration Post-MGNREGS implementation.

5.4 Findings of Hypotheses Testing

The Mahatma Gandhi National Rural Employment Guarantee Scheme (MGNREGS) provides 100 days employment to every rural household who are willing to work at the prevailing minimum wages. Therefore, it does not discriminate on the basis of socio-economic status of rural households in providing work. The present study hypothesizes that the socio-economic status of rural household does not influence the participation (employment) measured by average man-days in the scheme, addition to household income, access to bank credit & perception of rural households regarding assets created in the scheme. Besides, the present study hypothesized that MGNREGS has no effect on migration in the study area. The study has employed both parametric and non-parametric tools such as One Way ANOVA, Robust Test of Equality of means, Post-Hoc Test, t-Test and McNemar's Test for making proper inferences and generalisations.

The results suggest that there is a significant effect of socio-economic status of respondents on employment measured by average man-days and incomes of beneficiaries in the scheme. However, employment and addition to household income does not seem to vary between male and female respondents in the study area.

The mean scores on asset perception varies significantly across gender, social groups, income status but there is no significant difference in asset perception scores between marginal farmers, small farmers and landless labourers in the study area.

There is no significant influence of MGNREGS on access to bank credit in the study area after the scheme was implemented as was observed during hypothesis testing. Besides, the rural labour migration has significantly gone down post-MGNREGS implementation in the study area.

5.5 Policy Suggestions

Based on various observations in the present research study, the following policy suggestions targeting institutional issues, delivery mechanism and better outcomes from the scheme, could be put forward for effective and efficient implementation of the scheme in J&K and at National level.

Better Awareness on Rights & Entitlements in the Scheme: The effective delivery of scheme benefits can be achieved by ensuring that the target population is enriched with full and accurate information about the scheme. This could be done by ensuring better involvement of the GP, villagers and MGNREGS workers in generating quality awareness about the scheme. The Gram Sabha should be regularly held which could act as a platform to spread awareness about the benefits of MGNREGS. The information, education and communication (IEC) activities have to be undertaken to popularize the scheme and to bring awareness among the rural households & general public about citizens' rights & entitlements in the scheme. The targeted awareness campaigns by leveraging technology such as telecommunication etc. could go a long way in ensuring effective and efficient implementation of the scheme in the state and in the country.

Introduction of Work & Wage related Turn Around Time (TAT): The effective implementation and delivery of scheme benefits relies heavily on better execution of work and other activities. The high work incompletion rate year on year basis and enormous wage liability bill due to delayed payments to beneficiaries defeats the basic purpose of the scheme. Now, it is incumbent upon the policy makers to introduce the work & wage payment related process completion time, and setup a monitoring body for ensuring better accountability in case of deviations from the standard process time.

Asset Creation Based on Socio-economic Realities: The asset creation in the scheme should reflect ground realities in terms of relevance to the local economy. This could be achieved by following a 'bottom up approach' in works selection and estimation of budgets by incorporating the demands of the local population. The process could be further strengthened by establishing a robust quality management system by engaging professional monitors to ensure quality of durable assets created under MGNREGS. Besides, the higher inclusion of socially and economically disadvantaged groups in rural sector could ensure better outcomes from the scheme.

Worksite Facilities & Unemployment Allowance: The worksite facilities such as medical benefits, crèche facility for women, drinking and toilet facilities etc. are a right under MGNREGA Act (2005-06). However, the administration of worksite benefits has been poor for the entire history of the scheme in the study area as well as in the country at large, which is a violation of the Act. Therefore, for better implementation and compliance to Act guidelines the scheme benefits like worksite facilities and payment of unemployment allowance in the event of work is not provided to applicants should be strictly adhered to by implementation related stake holders and officials in the ministries in the State and at the Centre.

Differentiated Delivery: The continuous slashing of the budget allocation of funds for MGNREGS by central government is based on the neo-liberal economic arguments of minimal state intervention in providing social welfare to its people. The rationale that the massive budget allocations could be redeployed for better utilization in market driven environment although flawed in a democratic setup but it reignites the need to push for a differentiated delivery of employment and other benefits in the scheme. The differentiated delivery of scheme benefits could save a lot of money for the state exchequer, which could be utilized in other areas.

Therefore, slashing budget allocations for the scheme is not the right approach rather we should go for a differentiated delivery based on socio-economic status of rural households.

Adequate Staffing & Skill Enhancement of Functionaries: As per Section 18 of the MGNREGA, Act (2005-06) the State Governments are mandated to make available the district Programme Coordinator (PCs), Programme Officers (POs) and adequate staff and technical support as may be necessary for effective implementation of the scheme. The inadequate staff results in delayed work completion, faulty muster roll and other record keeping, delayed wage payments etc. which can be addressed only by adequate staffing of the scheme at all levels. Further, all who are involved with the planning and implementation under the scheme need some kind of skill set for better job performance. Which could be achieved by dequate training to POs, VLWs and officials of the PRIs. The specific problem in the state is adhoc and need based staffing policies which disincentivizes the better commitment and effort by the adhoc employees including Programme Officers (POs).

Transparency, Accountability & Convergence: For better implementation of the scheme and ensuring better outcomes from the scheme there is a urgent need of transparency, accountability and convergence with other rural sector schemes in the state and in India. The instrument of Social Audit would act as a catalyst in ensuring better transparency and accountability of various functionaries at all levels in the implementation framework. However, it has been seldom used and where ever it has been effectively utilized as in case of Andhra Pradesh, the scheme has shown tremendous success.

The convergence of MGNREGS with other schemes such as Sarva Siksha Abhiyan, RAMSA, Swach Bharat Abhiyan, Integrated Child Development Schemes and other state specific schemes could go a long in enhancing the combined impact of all these programmes in improving the socio-economic status of the target population in India in general and in J&K state in particular.

Scope for future Research

The observations from both primary and secondary data reveals that the operational performance of the scheme in the study area is satisfactory on some parameters such as financial inclusion, participation of women, SCs, STs, OBCs, awareness on entitlements, migration and access to credit where as it is dismal on other areas such as average days of employment and income, delayed wage payments, accountability and social audit. The study has focused on performance of the scheme separately in four block of Poonch and Kupwara district. The future research could further explore inclusion of other districts and blocks of the state for intra-regional and inter-regional comparisons in performance for better understanding of the operational efficacy of the scheme in J&K state. The present study has examined the effect of socio-economic status on participation (employment) and other variables such as addition to household income, access to bank credit and asset perception. There is a further scope for future research to explore other variables and examine the impact of MGNREGS on labour & other markets in the state.

Conclusion

The present study has endeavored to examine the operational performance of the scheme in four blocks of two districts in J&K state. The study has utilized both quantitative and qualitative data to capture the performance of the scheme on employment, income, income consumption pattern, migration, access to credit, asset perception, financial inclusion, awareness on entitlements and other implementation related issues.

The findings and observations from primary and secondary data indicates that various positive achievements in the scheme have been made such as on financial inclusion, inclusion of social and backward communities, women, utilization of funds and creation of durable assets. However, much is still to be desired as the full potential of MGNREGS in transforming rural economic landscape is yet to be realized. The real transformation can only happen in the rural sector when rural population is fully empowered through better and complete information about various rights and entitlements in the scheme, delivering on the expectations of socially and economically weaker sections of the rural communities, ensuring better transparency and accountability in the implementation of the scheme.

www.ingramcontent.com/pod-product-compliance
Lightning Source LLC
Chambersburg PA
CBHW030037230526
45472CB00002B/560